Mark Cholij

English
Basics

Practice & Revision

CAMBRIDGE
UNIVERSITY PRESS

CAMBRIDGE UNIVERSITY PRESS
Cambridge, New York, Melbourne, Madrid, Cape Town, Singapore,
São Paulo, Delhi, Dubai, Tokyo

Cambridge University Press
The Edinburgh Building, Cambridge CB2 8RU, UK

www.cambridge.org
Information on this title: www.cambridge.org/9780521648646

First published 1999
10th printing 2010

Printed in Dubai by Oriental Press

A catalogue record for this publication is available from the British Library

ISBN 978-0-521-64864-6 Paperback

Layout and composition by Newton Harris Design Partnership

Illustrations by Tim Sell

Contents

Introduction

This book forms part of a three-stage series that aims to cover the 'mechanics' of the English language (spelling, punctuation and grammar) at three graded levels. The emphasis in each of the three books is on practice and revision.

Each book offers a systematic work and study programme for use in the classroom or at home. Book 2 revises and builds upon the material covered in Book 1.

As the second book in the series, Book 2 has been written specifically for children in the 11–14 age group. As a revision manual, Book 2 is also suitable for older students who need to revise the general principles of English spelling, punctuation and grammar.

The book is equally suitable for students whose first language is not English. In broad terms, Book 2 is suitable for those students whose standard of English is at Cambridge First Certificate level or above.

Book 2 consists of thirty units, and each unit is divided into three sections. **Section A** consists of preliminary tasks which introduce the main topic and seek to establish the student's individual strengths and weaknesses. Having checked his/her answers to the preliminary tasks by referring to the key at the back of the book, the student is then directed to the **Reference** section. Having consulted the reference section, the student proceeds to **Section B** where the main topic is extended, revised and consolidated. A marking system is included in Section B for those students who wish to measure their progress.

Although the book is designed in such a way that one can dip in at random, it is recommended that students follow the order in which the units appear. This is especially important if the book is being used for individual study.

Guidance note for teachers/parents

The tasks in Section A of each unit are 'diagnostic' in nature. Students should not worry if they make a lot of mistakes in this section as they will have plenty of opportunity in Section B to show that they have learnt from their mistakes.

Glossary

Before starting this book, you should make sure that you are familiar with the following grammatical terms printed in bold:

1   The English alphabet has 26 letters, comprising five **vowels** (A, E, I, O, U) and twenty-one **consonants**.

2   A **noun** is a word used to name a person (e.g. Abdul), an object (e.g. a pen) or an abstract quality (e.g. honesty).

3   A **pronoun** (e.g. he, she, it) replaces a noun.

4   An **adjective** describes a noun (e.g. a *funny* story) or a pronoun (e.g. she is *tall*).

5   A **verb** indicates an action (e.g. he *ran* home) or a state (e.g. he *looks* sad).

6   The primary function of an **adverb** is to tell us more about a verb (e.g. he did it *quickly*) or an adjective (e.g. she is *really* clever).

7   **Prepositions** are words like *in*, *on*, *from*, *at* and *by* which are usually (but not always) found before a noun or pronoun.

8   A **sentence** is a set of words complete in itself and grouped together in such a way as to make complete sense. In written English, a sentence begins with a capital letter and ends with a full stop, a question mark (?) or an exclamation mark (!).

9   A **clause** is a group of words containing a verb. The following sentence consists of two clauses: 'If I see her tonight, I will give her the message.'
In the sentence above, 'I will give her the message' is the **main clause**. A main clause can stand on its own as an independent sentence.
'If I see her tonight' is a **subordinate** or **dependent** clause. A subordinate clause cannot stand on its own as an independent sentence.

10   A **prefix** is a word, a letter or a group of letters that we put at the beginning of a word to change its meaning. In the word *unusual*, for example, *un-* is a prefix meaning 'not'.

11   A **suffix** is a word, a letter or a group of letters that we put at the end of a word to form a new word. We can, for example, turn the verb *develop* into a noun by adding the suffix *-ment* (= development).

1 Capital letters

A

Task

In the jokes below, underline and correct any word that should start with a capital letter.

a an englishman, a scotsman and a welshman were stranded on a small island in the atlantic ocean. one day they found a magic lamp. when they rubbed it, a genie appeared and granted each of them one wish.
"i'd like to be back in birmingham," said the englishman. puff! he disappeared.
"i'd like to be back in glasgow," said the scotsman. puff! he disappeared.
"gosh," said the welshman, "i'm very lonely here on my own. i wish my friends were back again." puff! puff!

b my dad is the meanest person in the world. on christmas eve he fired his air-pistol outside our house. then he came in and told us that father christmas had committed suicide.

c in the days of oliver cromwell, a puritanical minister caught the young son of one of his flock fishing on a sunday.
"you wicked boy!" thundered the man of god. "don't you know it's a grave sin to fish on the sabbath?"
"i'm not fishing," protested the boy. "i'm just teaching my worm to swim!"

Now check your answers and then consult the **Reference** section before going on to **B**.

Reference

a A capital letter is used:

- to mark the beginning of a sentence and the start of direct speech
- with the specific names of people, places, events and organisations
- to show a person's title (e.g. Doctor Jones, Prince William)
- with abbreviations of names or titles
- with the days of the week, the months of the year, and festivals
- with the main words of a title (of a book, film, newspaper)
- to show nationality
- with languages and school subjects
- to write the pronoun 'I'

b Capitals are not necessary for the seasons of the year.

e.g. in summer, in autumn, in winter, in spring

c Be careful not to confuse normal *common* nouns with *proper* nouns (which begin with a capital letter). The particular name of a person, place or institution is classed as a *proper* noun. A *common* noun is a normal noun being used in a general sense.

e.g. Here are two common nouns:

He is a <u>doctor</u>. He works in a <u>hospital</u>.

Here are the same nouns being used as proper nouns:

Do you know <u>Dr Smith</u>? He works at <u>St George's Hospital</u>.

B

| Task |

In the following sentences, underline and correct those words that should start with a capital letter.

1 we asked our teacher whether king arthur had been a real king.

2 the pacific ocean is the largest ocean in the world.

3 when sir walter raleigh introduced tobacco into england in the early 1600s, king james I wrote a booklet arguing against its use.

4 the world's first underground railway was the metropolitan railway, which was opened in london in 1863.

5 on easter day in 1722, a dutch admiral called jacob roggeveen landed on a grass-covered island in the south pacific. he named it easter island.

6 my eldest brother is studying economics at essex university, but I don't want to go to university. when I leave school, I'm going to be a hairdresser.

7 she turned round and asked, "do you know which judge is trying the case? is it judge henson?"

8 "have you met professor oshima? he's a very famous professor from tokyo."

9 my french pen-friend is arriving at heathrow airport on monday 21 june.

10 my brother attends birchfield comprehensive school, but he doesn't like the school at all.

11 nuclear power was first produced by the italian scientist enrico fermi in the united states in 1942.

12 the longest canal able to take large sea-going ships is the suez canal. it passes through egypt to connect the mediterranean sea and the red sea.

Score: /12

2 Showing what someone has said

A

Task 1 Correct the joke below. Use capital letters, speech marks and other punctuation marks where appropriate.

my doctor has advised me to give up golf said fred

why asked his friend did he examine your heart

no replied fred but he had a look at my score card

Task 2 Punctuate the following sentences:

1 She said I'll see you later
2 I'll see you later she said
3 I'll see you tonight she said Don't forget to bring that book with you
4 I'll see you tonight she said and don't forget to bring that book with you

Task 3 Two of the four sentences below are wrongly punctuated. Which two?

1 He said, "I'm not feeling well."
2 He said, he was not feeling well.
3 She said, "I'm freezing."
4 She said that, she was freezing.

Now check your answers and then consult the **Reference** section before going on to **B**.

Reference

a We use speech marks to show the actual words spoken by someone (= direct speech). Speech marks may be single ('...') or double ("...").

b When creating a dialogue, we show that two people are speaking by putting their words on separate lines. Within the speech marks, we use the punctuation marks we would normally use for one sentence or more.

e.g.
"I've lost my dog."
"Why don't you put an advertisement in the paper?"
"Don't be silly! My dog can't read."

c Note, however, that a full stop becomes a comma if we add a phrase like *he said*:

e.g. "I've lost my dog," he said.

d Now look what happens when a phrase like *he said* is sandwiched between two pieces of direct speech:

(a) "I've lost my dog. What shall I do?" (two separate sentences) *becomes* "I've lost my dog," he said. "What shall I do?"

(b) "I've lost my dog, but I think I know where it is." (one sentence) *becomes* "I've lost my dog," he said, "but I think I know where it is."

e If we wish to introduce a piece of direct speech with a phrase like *he said*, we simply use a comma to separate the phrase from the words that were actually spoken. We must mark the beginning of direct speech with a capital letter even though the words may be in the middle of a sentence.

e.g. He said, "We will see you later."

Note: In a normal sentence where there are no speech marks, we never use a comma to separate phrases like *he said* or *she said that* from the words that follow.

e.g. He said he would do it later. / She said that she didn't like it.

B

Task

Correct the following pieces of writing. Use capital letters, speech marks and other punctuation marks where appropriate.

a anna shouted my teacher are you still with us

i nearly jumped out of my skin yes mrs jameson i answered

get on with your work then she said

b and where do you think you're going at this hour she demanded

we have to go out for a while susan replied we need

some fresh air

c urrgh said mr blenkins this lamb is really tough

i'm sorry said his wife but the butcher said it was a

spring lamb

then that explains it said mr blenkins i must be eating

one of the springs

Score: /20

3　The colon

. . . .

A

| Task |

Place a colon (:) where appropriate in the sentences below.

1　I can speak three languages French, Spanish and English.
2　The notice said 'Private. Keep out!'
3　There were only two ways he could have got out through the toilet window or the back door.
4　One evening, when slightly drunk, he broke the brutal news to her "Cynthia, I want this to be our last meeting. Carol and I are engaged …"
5　Everything had gone the jewels, the two gold watches, the silver cuff-links, the silk shirts.
6　Samir can't come with us he's not old enough.
7　There was still one problem how were we going to get back in time?
8　One person, the American inventor Thomas Midgley (1889–1944), created what are considered to be two of today's biggest environmental evils chlorofluorocarbons (CFCs) and leaded petrol.

Now check your answers and then consult the **Reference** section before going on to **B**.

Reference

a　It is not possible to link two separate sentences with a comma. It is possible, however, to join two separate sentences with a colon. The colon is a 'linking' punctuation mark that allows you to proceed with some kind of summary, illustration or direct explanation of what has just been stated. If you are unsure whether to use a colon or not, it might help to think of the colon as an equals sign (=).

e.g.　Lions are very lazy animals: they sleep for most of the day, and hunt at night.

I don't like Mark: he's so selfish.

b　A colon is also used to introduce an example, a quotation or a list of items.

e.g.　In his pocket they found the following items: a pistol, a knife and a passport.

Our teacher always uses the same proverb in class: 'more haste, less speed'.

c A colon may also be used instead of a comma to introduce direct speech.

e.g. While they were waiting for the police to arrive, he whispered to her: "Don't mention the money." She nodded and said: "Don't worry, I won't say anything."

d Unless direct speech is involved, the first word after a colon does not usually start with a capital letter. In American English, however, the first word after a colon usually begins with a capital letter.

B

Task 1 Put a colon where appropriate in the sentences below.

1 The whole area was dark and deserted no street lights, no house lights, nothing.

2 There was no doubt about it he was dead.

3 There was a sign on one of the doors 'Closed until further notice'.

4 She had been smoking marijuana and taking other drugs since she was thirteen. Now, said Mrs Turner, she had gone on to something worse heroin.

5 When I got to the top I saw a most spectacular sight five dragons were fighting five unicorns.

6 And then I had a happy thought there was no school tomorrow.

7 There were five rooms in the house three upstairs and two downstairs.

8 I recognised him immediately from the photos I had seen it was Boris Daggers, the famous sportsman.

Score: /8

Task 2 1 By taking out two words and using a colon, make the two sentences below into one sentence.

The rainbow has seven colours. They are red, orange, yellow, green, blue, indigo and violet.

2 By using a colon, reduce the piece of writing below from three sentences to two.

The dodo was a big flightless bird. There are no dodos left alive today. They are extinct.

3 By using a colon, reduce the piece of writing below from three sentences to two.

There is not much difference between rabbits and hares. They both have long ears and long back legs. Hares are slightly larger and move by jumping, whereas rabbits move by running.

Score: /3

4 The dash

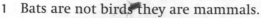

A

Task 1 Insert a dash (–) where appropriate in the sentences below.

1 Bats are not birds they are mammals.
2 He said he would do it and he did!
3 There was only one other customer an untidy, middle-aged man with a pair of binoculars slung over his shoulder.
4 And don't forget we leave in one hour.
5 He saw the red light in the middle of the road. It was being waved slowly up and down the international signal to stop.

Task 2 Insert dashes where appropriate in the sentences below.

1 Vitamin C which is essential for healthy teeth, gums and blood vessels can be found in fresh fruit and vegetables.
2 She and Reg had no secrets from each other. Well she laughed to herself only one ...
3 The speed of sound known as Mach 1, after the Austrian physicist and philosopher Ernst Mach is different at different heights.
4 The deepest lake in the world it is nearly a mile deep in places is Lake Baikal, in Siberia.
5 It wasn't too long ago 1977, to be exact that Cairo, a city of 8 million people, had only 208,000 telephones and no telephone directory.

Now check your answers and then consult the **Reference** section before going on to **B**.

Reference

a The dash is a very versatile punctuation mark. More often than not, a dash can be used in place of a comma, colon or semi-colon. It is also a fairly informal punctuation mark, and should not be overused in your writing. As you study the examples below, note that sometimes we need to use a pair of dashes and sometimes a single dash.

b We can use pairs of dashes (instead of commas or brackets) to mark an interruption within a sentence.

e.g. And then Henry – who's as strong as an ox – arrived on the scene, and together we managed to chase the gang away.

c   We can use pairs of dashes to emphasise a word or phrase.

e.g.   If the human appendix becomes inflamed, it has to be taken out –
fast – by what is nowadays a simple operation.

d   When adding an explanation or introducing a list, we can use a
dash instead of a colon.

e.g.   I found the exam extremely difficult – half the questions were
impossible!

e   Before an afterthought (in informal English), we use a dash.

e.g.   I sent Henry an invitation – at least, I think I did!

f   To create a dramatic pause, we can use a dash.

e.g.   I looked up – and saw Stella with a gun in her hand.
I looked up and saw Stella – with a gun in her hand.

B

| Task 1 | Insert dashes where appropriate in the sentences below.

1   Even at that early hour it was not yet six o'clock he was
immaculately dressed.
2   Everything that we know about dinosaurs and everything that
we will ever know comes from fossils.
3   An unusual thing about the spotted hyena is that unlike most
animals the female is larger than the male.
4   How could you speak to him your own father in such a way?
5   Even my brother who is not known for his sense of humour
had to laugh when I told him what had happened.   Score: /5

| Task 2 | Insert a dash where appropriate in the sentences below.

1   The longest jump that has ever been recorded was a great
bound of forty-two feet made by a kangaroo back in 1951
though, of course, it cannot be proved that there have not been
even longer unrecorded ones.
2   He was a tall, lean man with thinning hair and a pleasant face
the kind of face one would find hard to remember.
3   He smiled again a cold, hard smile.
4   An iceberg larger than Belgium was observed in the South
Pacific in 1956. It was 208 miles long and 60 miles wide the
largest ever seen.
5   The longest underwater cable is nine thousand miles long, and
it runs all the way from Australia to Port Alberni, Canada. It is
known as COMPAC the Commonwealth Pacific Cable.   Score: /5

13

5 The comma 1

A

Task 1 Insert commas where appropriate in the joke below.

Traveller:	Excuse me do you have a room for tonight?
Hotel proprietor:	Certainly sir. It'll be £50 a night or I can let you have a room for only £10 if you make your own bed.
Traveller:	I'll take the £10 room.
Hotel proprietor:	Right! I'll just go and fetch the wood the hammer and the nails for the bed ...

Task 2 Place a comma where appropriate in each of the sentences below.

1 According to Yoko Fusako intends to sell her cottage and move back to the city.
2 Being rich he doesn't need to work for a living.
3 Then she fumbled with the matches lit the gas-ring and put the kettle on to boil.
4 If air is blown into water bubbles rise to the surface.
5 With the possible exception of the cobra crocodiles kill more people than any other animal.

Now check your answers and then consult the **Reference** section before going on to **B**.

Reference

a In the same way that a full stop prevents one sentence from running into another, so too a comma prevents words within a sentence from running into each other.

b We use a comma between items in a list. We do not usually place a comma before the final *and/or* in a list of items.

e.g. We had chips, sausages, bacon and peas for lunch. / You can have an apple, a banana or a pear.

c We also use commas to separate a series of verbs that have the same subject.

e.g. He walked into the room, said hello, poured himself a drink and sat down.

d Words that form part of an introduction to the main message of the sentence are usually marked off by a comma.

e.g. Not feeling well, she decided to stay at home. / Actually, I'm not late!

e If we begin a sentence with such words as *although*, *despite*, *if*, *when*, *after*, *before*, *as soon as*, *just as*, *as*, *while*, etc., we should use a comma before beginning the main part of the sentence.

e.g. <u>Despite</u> the weather, we had a great time. / <u>If</u> it rains, we will watch a video.

On the other hand, a comma is usually quite unnecessary if the main part of the sentence comes first.

e.g. We had a great time <u>despite</u> the weather. / We'll watch a video <u>if</u> it rains.

f When joining clauses, there is nothing wrong with using a comma before such 'joining' words as *and*, *but*, *or*, *so* if this helps to make the sentence more balanced and clearer to the reader.

e.g. We talked for a while, and then she stood up and took her suitcase off the rack.
She pretended she was a doctor, but we weren't fooled.
The meal was really disgusting, so we left the restaurant without paying.

B

Task

Insert commas where appropriate in the sentences below.

1 The giraffe is the tallest of all living animals but scientists are unable to explain how it got its long neck.
2 She opened the parcel saw what was inside and let out a loud scream.
3 To my astonishment and delight I was awarded first prize in the competition.
4 We yawn when we are tired sleepy or bored.
5 If they are not here by seven we shall start without them.
6 One of the things that birds snakes frogs cows and humans all have in common is a backbone.
7 Even after their heads have been cut off some insects may live for as long as a year. They react automatically to light temperature humidity chemicals and other stimuli.
8 According to legend a mermaid is a young girl who lives in the sea. Instead of legs she has the tail of a fish.
9 With the exception of the organ the piano is the most complex musical instrument.
10 Although I have been to France several times I do not speak French.

Score: /16

15

6 The comma 2

A

Task

In which of the following sentences do we need commas? Add commas where necessary. How many commas are required: one or two? Tick any sentence that does not require a comma.

1 One type of spider the tarantula eats birds and can live as long as 15 years.
2 The one type of spider that nearly everybody fears is the tarantula.
3 The tallest living animal is the giraffe which lives in Africa.
4 The animal which most closely resembles man is the ape.
5 A bird is a creature which has feathers and wings.
6 The peregrine falcon which is the fastest bird in the world can reach speeds of 217 miles per hour.
7 He told us that he did not have any money which was definitely not true.
8 Mr Khan who usually deals with these matters is away on holiday.
9 The person who usually deals with such matters is away on holiday.
10 The donkey which was domesticated more than 5,000 years ago by the Egyptians is one of the earliest animals used in agriculture.

Now check your answers and then consult the **Reference** section before going on to **B**.

Reference

a Any interruption in a sentence should normally be marked off by commas. An interruption may be in the form of one word or more.

There are, however, other ways of dealing with the problem.
My neighbour, a keen gardener, helped me to plant the rose bushes.

(An interruption in a sentence can also be marked off by dashes. See Unit 4.)

b The most frequent type of interruption is one that adds extra information to the main message of the sentence (= the main clause).

● We use two commas (like two brackets) to enclose any words that are not essential to the main message of the sentence.

If we were to take those words out, the rest of the sentence would still make sense.

- On the other hand, we must never mark off words that are essential to the main message of the sentence.

e.g.   Mr Evans, who has been teaching for forty years, retires next month.
Anybody who has been teaching for forty years deserves a medal!
I need to talk to someone who works in a restaurant.
My brother, who happens to work in a restaurant, may be able to help you.

c   We use one comma (like a dash) to mark off any additional information/comment that follows the main clause.

e.g.   He arrived early, which surprised us all.

B

Task

Insert commas where appropriate in the sentences below. Tick any sentence that does not require commas.

1   Among the most important peoples of ancient America were the Aztecs who lived in the valley which now contains Mexico City.
2   I'd like you to meet the man who saved my life.
3   The Vatican City which is the official home of the Pope is the world's smallest country.
4   Penicillin which was discovered by Alexander Fleming has saved millions of lives.
5   Silver which is the commonest precious metal is lighter than gold.
6   The human body has 636 muscles each with its own name.
7   The St Gotthard tunnel which runs beneath the Swiss Alps is the world's longest road tunnel.
8   The exam that we took this morning was dead easy.
9   A machine that washes dishes is called a dishwasher.
10   He wanted to give all his money to charity which seemed very reasonable to me.
11   I gave her the watch that I had found in the street.
12   The woman you were talking to is a very famous actress.
13   The 'Mona Lisa' which was painted by Leonardo da Vinci is the most easily recognised painting in the world.
14   My father who used to be a businessman is training to be a bus driver.

Score: /14

7 Making nouns plural

A

Task | Make the nouns below plural.
e.g.   boy/boys

1 dish - bus - cactus - tax - taxi - oasis
2 kilo - video - hero - photo - tomato - piano
3 loaf - thief - chief - shelf - knife - cliff
4 lorry - copy - delay - enquiry - kidney - lady
5 son-in-law - passer-by - runner-up
6 tooth - goose - sheep - ox - louse
7 stratum - medium - phenomenon - bureau - series

Now check your answers and then consult the **Reference** section before going on to **B**.

Reference

a To make most nouns plural, simply add *-s* (not *-'s*):

e.g. place/places; ski/skis; pen/pens

b Add *-es* to words ending in *-ch*, *-sh*, *-s*, *-ss*, *-x*. These are known as sibilant (= 'hissing') consonants, and an *e* is required to ease pronunciation.

e.g. benches, coaches, brushes, dishes, gases, dresses, boxes, foxes

Exceptions (1): loch/lochs; stomach/stomachs
(2): oasis/oases; crisis/crises
(3): cactus/cacti *or* cactuses; radius/radii *or* radiuses; fungus/fungi *or* funguses (Both plural forms are acceptable.)

c For most words ending in *-o*, simply add *-s*. This is especially true of words that end in a vowel + *-o*, and words that are abbreviations of longer words.

e.g. cellos, pianos, radios, ratios, zoos, cuckoos, hippos, photos

Exceptions (1): tomatoes, potatoes, echoes, dominoes, heroes
(2): mosquito(e)s, tornado(e)s, volcano(e)s, mango(e)s
(These words can end in either *-s* or *-es*.)

d For words ending in a consonant + *-y*, change the *-y* to *-i* and add *-es*:

e.g. baby/babies; story/stories; city/cities

e For words ending in a vowel + *-y*, simply add *-s*:

e.g. journey/journeys; monkey/monkeys; ray/rays

f For words ending in *-f* or *-fe*, change the *-f* or *-fe* to *-ves*:

loaf/loaves; leaf/leaves; half/halves; knife/knives

Exceptions (1): chiefs, handkerchiefs, roofs, cliffs
(2): dwarfs *or* dwarves; scarfs *or* scarves;
hoofs *or* hooves
(These words may end in either *-fs* or *-ves*.)

g Particular attention should be paid to the following words of foreign origin:

phenomenon/phenomena; stratum/strata; medium/media; chateau/chateaux; bureau/bureaux; gateau/gateaux (It is also possible to use *-s* instead of *-x* for the last three words.)

h Be careful with certain words that have hyphens:

e.g. passers-by; sons-in-law; lay-bys

i Some words do not change at all. They are both singular and plural.

e.g. species; series; sheep; deer; salmon

j Some plural words need to be learnt separately.

e.g. man/men; foot/feet; goose/geese; tooth/teeth; louse/lice; mouse /mice; ox/oxen

B

| Task |

Make the following nouns plural:

1 radius - church - coach - fungus - crisis - kiss - witch   Score: /7

2 kangaroo - echo - patio - potato - cello - rhino - mosquito   Score: /7

3 life - wife - shelf - roof - leaf - handkerchief - scarf - calf   Score: /8

4 valley - city - story - journey - apology - strawberry - dictionary   Score: /7

5 jockey - country - storey - turkey - butterfly - fairy - body   Score: /7

6 salmon - child - deer - woman - mouse   Score: /5

7 chateau - species - gateau - brother-in-law   Score: /4

8   Singular or plural?

A

Task

Select the correct alternative in brackets.

1 A number of students (has / have) been suspended.
2 The number of students attending the school (have / has) increased from 500 to 600.
3 One in six people (suffer / suffers) from insomnia.
4 One of the children (have / has) caught malaria.
5 I am sure it (were / was) you who told me about Mary.
6 It (were / was) the strawberries that made her ill.
7 There (were / was) a lot of people at the party.
8 There (is / are) two biscuits left. Do you want one?
9 (Has / Have) everybody left the building?
10 Neither of my parents (drives / drive).
11 Both of them (is / are) taking driving lessons.
12 Most of my luggage (is / are) still missing.
13 The news (was / were) better than expected.
14 The scissors (is / are) on the table.
15 Ten miles (is / are) a long way to walk!
16 Each of my brothers (has / have) his own room.
17 My family (was / were) delighted with their presents.
18 The crew (was / were) tired after their long flight.
19 Gymnastics (was / were) my favourite activity at school.

Now check your answers and then consult the **Reference** section before going on to **B**.

Reference

a We normally use a singular verb with these kinds of words:

- it / one (of) / each (of) / every / nobody / no one / everybody / everyone / anybody / anyone / neither (of) / either (of)
- furniture / information / rubbish / luggage
- Mathematics / Physics / athletics / gymnastics / measles / news

b We use a singular verb when describing an amount or quantity:

e.g. Six months is a long time to be off school.

c We use a singular verb with *neither...nor* / *either...or* if there are just two people or things involved. If one of the nouns is plural, then the verb agrees with the nearer noun.

e.g.   Neither Mary nor James <u>was</u> invited to the party. / Neither Mary nor her friends <u>were</u> invited to the party. / Neither the twins nor John <u>was</u> invited.

d   We can use either a singular verb or a plural verb for many 'group' nouns (e.g. family, team, class, club, public, government, committee, school, company, firm, staff, crew, orchestra, choir). Your choice of verb will depend on whether you are viewing the group as a whole (= as a single unit) or as a number of individuals in a group. The important point is to be consistent with accompanying words such as *it* or *they*.

e.g.   The jury <u>has</u> reached <u>its</u> verdict. / The jury <u>are</u> still discussing the case. <u>They</u> have been out for ten hours.

e   We use a plural verb for the following words:

scissors, trousers, police, people

f   We use a plural verb with 'a number of ...', and a singular verb with 'the number of ...'.

g   If *there* + verb introduces a singular noun (on its own, or the first of a list), the verb will be singular. If *there* + verb introduces a plural noun, the verb will be plural.

e.g.   There is a pen on your desk. / There's a pen, two rubbers and a pencil on your desk. / There are two pens, a rubber and a pencil on your desk.

B

| Task | Select the correct alternative in brackets. |

1 Either Sharon or Tracey (is / are) lying.
2 There (is / are) hundreds of people outside!
3 Fortunately, neither of the drivers (was / were) injured.
4 Apparently, neither Craig nor Ian (wants / want) to help.
5 Each of those instruments (costs / cost) over £1,000.
6 Everybody (was / were) surprised at her attitude.
7 A number of books (is / are) missing from the library.
8 The number of people who (has / have) died in road accidents (has / have) doubled in the past year.
9 All the furniture in this room (is / are) antique.
10 Every animal and plant (eats / eat), or (is / are) eaten by, other things.
11 There (is / are) plenty of activities for the young in this centre.
12 Physics (is / are) my worst subject at school.
13 The team (is / are) training twice as hard this week because they are playing the league champions on Saturday.
14 There (is / are) a kitchen, a dining-room and a toilet downstairs.

Score: /16

9   The apostrophe 1

A

Task 1

Read the following joke and put in the missing apostrophes.

A man went for a brain transplant and was offered the choice of two brains – an architects for £100 and a politicians for £10,000. "Does that mean that the politicians brain is much better than the architects?" asked the man.
"Not exactly," replied the brain transplant salesman. "Its just that the politicians brain has never been used."

Task 2

How many mistakes can you find below? Underline and correct them.

1   Shes emigrating to Australia in two years' time.
2   In the 1960s, she attended a girl's grammar school.
3   I spent the night at my gran's. Thats the truth!
4   Mary's uncle does'nt like me at all.
5   Mr Jones' secretary is five months' pregnant.
6   She's eaten all our sweet's!
7   Ann: Now that were engaged, I hope youll give me a ring.
    Norman: Of course I will. Whats your number?

Now check your answers and then consult the **Reference** section before going on to **B**.

Reference

a We use the apostrophe + -*s* to show a 'possessive' or 'belonging' relationship between two nouns.

e.g. my sister's bedroom; my brother's friend

b It is sometimes possible to leave out the second noun in a 'possessive' phrase.

e.g. to go to the doctor's (= to go to the doctor's surgery)

We may leave out the second noun in order to avoid unnecessary repetition.

e.g. Paula's story is more interesting than Fiona's.

c If the first noun in a possessive relationship already has an -*s*, we simply add an apostrophe to show that it is a plural noun.

e.g. the boy's pyjamas (We are talking about one boy.)
       the boys' pyjamas (We are talking about more than one boy.)

If a plural noun does not end in -s (e.g. women, men, children, people), we treat it like a normal noun and add apostrophe + -s.

e.g.   Women's clothes tend to be more expensive than men's.

d If a singular noun (usually the name of a person) ends in -s, you can add either -'s or just an apostrophe.

e.g.   Doris's hat / Doris' hat // Mr Jones's car / Mr Jones' car

For longer words, it is best just to use an apostrophe after the -s.

e.g.   Mr Jenkins is married. / Mr Jenkins' children are married.

e We use the apostrophe in phrases showing duration of time.

e.g.   a fortnight's holiday; in a year's time; in two months' time

Note: We do not use the apostrophe in time phrases if the last word is an adjective.

e.g.   He is six years old. / She is seven months pregnant.

f We use the apostrophe when contracting words (= making two words into one). The apostrophe must be placed where the missing letter(s) should be.

e.g.   we do not = we don't; they are = they're; I will = I'll

g The apostrophe is used to form the plurals of letters and numbers.

e.g.   Dot the i's and cross the t's. / Three 3's are nine.

For numbers over nine, it is up to you whether to use an apostrophe or not.

e.g.   in the 1930s / in the 1930's

B

| Task |

Place apostrophes where appropriate in the sentences below.

1 Theyve gone off to Rome for a fortnights holiday.
2 They said theyd see us in two weeks time.
3 We took Mrs Browns dog to the vets this morning.
4 Heres the ladies cloakroom, and the mens is over there.
5 Theres a storm coming. Wed better take shelter.
6 "It wasnt Aichas fault!" I shouted. "She couldnt help it."
7 Have you met the Smiths? Theyre from York.
8 Lets pop down to the newsagents.
9 My parents house was sold for a hundred thousand pounds.
10 Dimitris mother doesnt approve of the way I dress.
11 Thats not my sons coat! Wheres James jacket?
12 "I think well paint the childrens bedroom first," she said.   Score: /12

10   The apostrophe 2

Task

A

Task Choose the correct alternative in the brackets below.

1 (Whose / Who's) turn is it?
2 (Whose / Who's) watch is it?
3 (Whose / Who's) got my watch?
4 (Your / You're) Andrew's English teacher, aren't you?
5 (Your / You're) English teacher is not pleased with you, Andrew.
6 Psychiatrist: What is your problem?
   Patient: I prefer long socks to short socks.
   Psychiatrist: So what? Lots of people do. Even I do.
   Patient: Really? What a relief! How do you like (yours / your's)
                  – fried or boiled?
7 "Our cat has lost (its / it's) appetite."
   "So has (ours / our's). It won't eat (its / it's) food."
8 (Its / It's) extremely valuable. In fact, (its / it's) worth (its / it's)
   weight in gold.
9 That isn't Melinda's coat. (Hers / Her's) is pale green.
10 (Their / They're / There) always late!
11 (There's / Theirs) nothing left to eat.
12 Do you want to be in our team or in (there's / theirs)?
13 One should follow (ones / one's) instincts.

Now check your answers and then consult the **Reference** section before going on to **B**.

Reference

a Some words do not require an apostrophe to show that they are
'possessive'. Be particularly careful with the spelling of possessive
<u>adjectives</u> (= *whose, my, your, his, her, its, our, their*) and possessive
<u>pronouns</u> (= *mine, yours, his, hers, ours, theirs*).

b Certain words sound alike and are often confused. Note carefully
the following:
  ● *whose / who's*
     Whose car is it? = Who does the car belong to? (possessive)
     Who's in the car? = Who is in the car?
     Who's taken my car? = Who has taken my car?
  ● *your / you're*
     Is this your coat? = Does this coat belong to you? (possessive)
     You're wearing my coat. = You are wearing my coat.

- *there | their | they're*
  There it is! (*there* is the opposite of *here*)
  It's their ball. = The ball belongs to them. (possessive)
  They're here. = They are here.
- *there's | theirs*
  There's something wrong. = There is something wrong.
  It's not theirs. = It does not belong to them. (possessive)
- *it's | its*
  It's green. = It is green. | It's been raining. = It has been raining.
  The school wants to change its image. (*its* = possessive; the
  image belongs to the school)

c In formal English, we can use *one* to mean *you* (in general). To make
one possessive we add apostrophe + *-s*:

One shouldn't waste one's time. = You shouldn't waste your time.

B

Task 1

Replace the underlined words with a single possessive pronoun.
e.g. It is <u>my pen</u>. = It is <u>mine</u>.

1 My pen is not working. Can I borrow <u>your pen</u>?
2 His bedroom is larger than <u>her bedroom</u>.
3 Her bedroom is tidier than <u>his bedroom</u>.
4 Our garden is smaller than <u>their garden</u>.
5 Their garden is prettier than our garden.   Score: /5

Task 2

Correct the sentences below.

1 Its a depressing day. Its cold and the skys overcast.
2 Whats wrong, Timothy? Your shaking like a leaf.
3 Whose that man dressed in black? And whose he talking to?
4 Its difficult to say whose to blame. I'm not sure whose fault it
   is.
5 If this pen isn't your's, then who's is it?
6 A woodpecker uses it's beak to peck at wood.
7 They're welcome to come with us, but theirs no room for
   there luggage.
8 Well, to be frank, I think one should mind ones own business.
9 As long as one tries ones best, theirs no shame in failure.
10 Fry it until its skin is golden brown. Its best to serve it while
   its piping hot.   Score: /10

11 Two words in one

A

| Task |

How many spelling mistakes can you find in the sentences below?
Underline and correct each mistake.

1　Eloise is a skillful tennis player.
2　You look cheerfull! Have you received some good news?
3　Add a spoonfull of sugar to the ingredients and stir well.
4　She said that he was wellcome to her share of the money.
5　Allthough she is disabled, she leads a fairly normall life.
6　His grandaughter visits him occasionally.
7　It is a crime to withold information from the police.
8　Chimpanzees are playfull creatures.
9　Parents are responsible for the wellfare of their children.
10　She said she was gratefull for his help.
11　She warned the teacher that Giovanni was a willful child.

Now check your answers and then consult the **Reference** section before going on to **B**.

Reference

a　When a word ends in -*ll*, it usually loses one *l* when it is joined to another word.

e.g.　all + most = almost; well + come = welcome; power + full = powerful; care + full = careful; beauty + full = beautiful

(Note that consonant + -*y* becomes consonant + -*i* when joined to *full*.)

b　When two words ending in -*ll* are joined together, they both lose one *l*.

e.g.　skill + full = skilful; full + fill = fulfil; will + full = wilful

c　Do not confuse adjectives with adverbs. To form an adverb, one usually adds -*ly* to an adjective. Accordingly, adjectives that end in -*ful* will end in -*fully* when they become adverbs.

e.g.　painful, painfully; cheerful, cheerfully

d　If two words are joined by a hyphen, a word ending in -*ll* does not change to a single *l*.

e.g.　well-off, well-known, all-out, all-round, full-time, ill-advised

You should also note that -*ll* is retained in certain 'compound' words. A compound word is a word formed from other words.

e.g.　overall, farewell, fullback

e When two words are put together to make a compound word, the words usually remain complete.

e.g. with + hold = withhold; grand + daughter = granddaughter; over + rate = overrate; over + ride = override; pass + word = password

Exceptions: grand + dad = grandad *or* granddad; pass + time = pastime

If in doubt when joining two words, use a hyphen.

e.g. earring *or* ear-ring

B

Task 1

Complete each sentence with the correct form of the word in brackets.
e.g. We had a .... time. (wonder) ➜ wonderful

1 He was a .... king and forgave her. (mercy)
2 I hope you will be .... (succeed)
3 What a .... baby! (beauty)
4 We felt sorry for him: he looked so .... (pity)
5 Please be more .... in future! (care)

Score: /5

Task 2

How many spelling mistakes can you find in the sentences below?
Underline and correct each mistake.

1 Jericho, in Jordan, is the oldest town in the world. People have lived there for allmost ten thousand years.
2 I have allready told her that she is not welcome here.
3 The Sun's harmfull ultra-violet rays are filtered out by the ozone layer.
4 Going for a walk in the park is a traditional family passtime.
5 We have informed him that he must fullfil his obligations.
6 It was a delight to watch such a skillfull and gracefull dancer.
7 I am not alltogether happy with their decision.
8 Her granson can be a bit of a handfull at times.
9 You are not allowed to wear earings at school.
10 Two old ladies were saying farewel to their beloved vicar who was moving on to another parish.
"We shall miss you ever so much, vicar," said the first lady in a sorrowfull voice. "And we shall especially miss your sermons."
"Oh yes, we shall indeed," agreed the second tearfuly. "We never knew what sin really was untill you came here."

Score: /15

12 One word or (maybe / may be) two?

A

Task

Choose the correct alternative in brackets.

1 Are you (all right / alright)?
2 I have (all ready / already) seen that film.
3 They were (all ready / already) and waiting when I arrived.
4 That will be £23 (all together / altogether).
5 Don't separate them. Keep them (all together / altogether).
6 Fortunately, (no one / noone) was injured.
7 Has (any one / anyone) seen my blue sweater?
8 I don't mind. (Any one / Anyone) of them will do.
9 When the alarm went off, (every one / everyone) panicked.
10 I see her (every day / everyday).
11 I have two jackets. This one is for (every day / everyday) use.
12 I (may be / maybe) late tomorrow morning.
13 She (can not / cannot) read or write.
14 Is there (any way / anyway) of contacting her?
15 (Any way / Anyway), I don't have time to discuss this now.
16 (Thank you / Thankyou) for the lovely present.
17 I like him (a lot / alot).
18 He won a (gold fish / goldfish) at the fair.

Now check your answers and then consult the **Reference** section before going on to **B**.

Reference

a Although some people prefer *alright* to *all right*, the fact remains that only *all right* is acceptable in standard written English.

b Look carefully at the words underlined below. Where one word is used, note the explanation in brackets. Where two words have been used, this means that they are two separate words of equal value. In each case, the grammar of the sentence tells us whether to use one word or two.

1 They have <u>already</u> gone. (an adverb)
They are <u>all</u> <u>ready</u> to carry out your orders.

2 I was not <u>altogether</u> satisfied with her reply. (= 'entirely')
I would prefer to see them <u>all</u> <u>together</u>, not separately.

3 <u>Anyone</u> could have taken it. (= 'anybody')
<u>Any</u> <u>one</u> of those students could have taken it.

4 Is <u>everyone</u> here? (= 'everybody')
Look at these sentences. <u>Every one</u> of them is wrong!

5 Burglary is an <u>everyday</u> occurrence. (an adjective)
I go jogging <u>every day</u>.

6 <u>Maybe</u> I ought to tell the police. (= 'perhaps')
They <u>may be</u> in Australia.

7 <u>Anyway</u>, what does it matter? (= 'anyhow')
Is there <u>any way</u> of raising more money before the deadline?

8 I didn't even get a <u>thank-you</u>. (*or* thankyou) (a noun)
I sent her a <u>thank-you</u> (*or* thankyou) letter. (an adjective)
<u>Thank you</u> very much for all that you have done.

c The negative form of *can* is *can't* or *cannot* (one word).

d The following are written as two words: *no one* (= 'nobody'); *in case*;
a lot; *in front*; *as well*.

e Be careful not to confuse a compound noun (e.g. a goldfish) with an
adjective and noun (e.g. a gold fish = 'a fish made of gold').

B

Choose the correct alternative in brackets.

1 I was not (all together / altogether) surprised.
2 It doesn't matter which book. (Any one / Anyone) will do.
3 You can take (any one / anyone) of these cakes.
4 Did (any one / anyone) see what actually happened?
5 (Every one / Everyone) of these pictures is a fake.
6 There's (no one / noone) here. (Every one / Everyone) has gone.
7 She visits her grandmother (every day / everyday).
8 You are not going (all ready / already), are you?
9 If you are (all ready / already), we shall begin.
10 (May be / Maybe) I'll see her tonight.
11 I (may be / maybe) able to help her.
12 There (may be / maybe) trouble ahead.
13 Is there (any way / anyway) we can help?
14 I just wanted to (thank you / thankyou) for all your help.
15 She sat (in front / infront) of us.
16 Take a jacket (in case / incase) it gets cold.
17 I am sorry, but I (can not / cannot) stand her!
18 He has gone to the local (super market / supermarket).
19 "This is Sue, my (flat mate / flatmate)."

Score: /20

13 The hyphen

A

Task 1
Complete the definitions below.
> e.g. hair that reaches down to one's shoulders = shoulder-length hair

1 a boy with fair hair =
2 a girl who is twelve years old =
3 a flight that lasts eight hours =
4 a course that lasts three months =
5 a journey that takes two days =
6 a man who looks suspicious =
7 eyes that look sad =

Task 2
In which of the following cases is a hyphen necessary?

1 my great grandfather	5 a hold up
2 a swimming pool	6 forty four chairs
3 a break in	7 his ex wife
4 a waiting room	8 a non smoker

Now check your answers and then consult the **Reference** section before going on to **B**.

Reference

a A hyphen shows that we wish to treat two or more words as a single unit. A single unit formed of two or more words is known as a 'compound' word.

e.g. brother-in-law; X-ray; ice-skating; washing-up

b There are no fixed rules for using the hyphen with compound <u>nouns</u>. These may be written as one word (e.g. motorway), as two words (e.g. safety pin), or with a hyphen (e.g. lamp-post).

Quite often it is a question of personal choice (e.g. by-pass or bypass). An unfamiliar or confusing combination of words will, however, usually require a hyphen. We use a hyphen, for example, to distinguish between certain nouns and verbs (e.g. a take-away / to take away).

On the other hand, a familiar, straightforward combination of words will not usually require a hyphen.

e.g. a shoe shop; a school teacher; a department store; a farm worker

c We often use a hyphen with certain prefixes. A prefix is a word or set of letters placed in front of a word.

e.g. <u>anti</u>-smoking; <u>co</u>-operative; <u>ex</u>-boyfriend; <u>mid</u>-air crash; <u>non</u>-stop

d A compound <u>adjective</u> requires a hyphen.

e.g. broken-hearted; big-headed

Any compound number (between 20 and 100) also requires a hyphen.

Note: With compound nouns, we can often choose whether to use a hyphen or not.

e.g. a swimming pool / a swimming-pool; a dining room / a dining-room

If we use these words as adjectives, we have no choice.

e.g. a swimming-pool attendant; a dining-room table

e Very often a group of words can <u>only</u> be used as a compound adjective when placed <u>before</u> a noun.

e.g. an out-of-work actor = the actor is out of work / a well-known actress = the actress is well known for her acting

B

| Task | Supply hyphens where appropriate in the sentences below. |

1 Mr Hook is an ill tempered, pig headed, hard hearted secondary school teacher.
2 She was wearing a white hat and a silver coloured dress.
3 He was a grey bearded, middle aged man with a reddish face.
4 With Peter was a rather thick set, pleasant looking man in his mid thirties.
5 He was a tall one eyed man with a serious looking face.
6 She gave me some home baked cake and a glass of fresh orange juice.
7 Cyrano de Bergerac, seventeenth century poet, wit and expert swordsman, fought and won at least one thousand duels over insults about his extra large nose. During one three month period, he 'ran through' four people each week.
8 Anna's husband to be is a hard headed businessman who owns a multi storey car park near the town centre.
9 "I am fed up with being treated like a ten year old child!" complained Bouchra. "I am actually eleven years old!"
10 Father to son: "I know there's a big crack in the sitting room wall, but that's no reason to go telling everyone that you come from a broken home."

Score: /10

14 Some troublesome nouns

A

Task 1 To complete each sentence below, form a noun ending in -*ness* or -*ment* from the word in brackets.

1 Many elderly people suffer from .... (lonely)
2 He was given no .... (encourage)
3 He is well known for his .... (mean)
4 Are they having another .... ? (argue)
5 I am sure she'll get over her .... (shy)
6 His .... really annoys me. (lazy)

Task 2 To complete each sentence below, form a noun ending in -*tion* from the word in brackets.

1 Are you going to enter the swimming .... ? (compete)
2 He needs to improve his .... (pronounce)
3 The place had changed beyond .... (recognise)
4 She demanded an .... (explain)
5 She gave the police a detailed .... of the man. (describe)
6 His proposals met with a lot of .... (oppose)

Now check your answers and then consult the **Reference** section before going on to **B**.

Reference

a When forming nouns with -*ment*, it is important to remember that we usually keep -*e* before -*ment*.

 e.g.   excite - exciting - excit<u>e</u>ment

Exception: argue - arguing - arg<u>u</u>ment

b When forming nouns with -*ness*, remember that -*y* will usually change to -*i*.

 e.g.   nasty - nastiness; tidy - tidiness; happy - happiness

Exceptions: dryness, shyness

c When we add -*ness* to a word ending in -*n*, we will end up with *nn* in the middle of the word.

 e.g.   openness, meanness, drunkenness

Note: A female lion = a lioness (= lion + -*ess*).

d Certain nouns ending in *-tion* are tricky to spell for a variety of reasons. It is best to learn the following words by heart:

- deceive - deception; describe - description; receive - reception
- abolish - abolition; add - addition; compete - competition; define - definition; oppose - opposition; recognise - recognition; repeat - repetition
- abbreviate - abbreviation; accommodate - accommodation; accuse - accusation; assassinate - assassination; associate - association; cancel - cancellation; despair - desperation; exaggerate - exaggeration; explain - explanation; imagine - imagination; pronounce - pronunciation; separate - separation

B

Task 1

To complete each sentence below, form a noun ending in *-ness* or *-ment* from the word in brackets.

1 He assured her that her (happy) was his prime concern.
2 We were impressed by the (friendly) of the hotel staff.
3 He was proud of his (achieve).
4 He gave a lecture on the (ugly) of modern architecture.
5 In his (excite), he forgot to leave his name and address.
6 When taking this medicine, some people may experience the following side-effects: (dizzy) and (dry) in the mouth.

Score: /7

Task 2

Most of the sentences below contain one spelling mistake. Underline and correct each mistake. Tick any sentence that does not contain a spelling mistake.

1 There is too much repeatition in this essay.
2 There was a look of desparation in her eyes.
3 There is a shortage of cheap accomodation.
4 They will have to pay a cancelation fee.
5 It is no exageration to say that I owe her my life.
6 She told him that he had a vivid imagination.
7 The explaination was crystal clear.
8 A dictionary gives you defenitions of words.
9 In adittion to his salary, he receives a yearly bonus.
10 The visitors were given a warm reception by their hosts.
11 He was horrified by her acussation.
12 Even a short period of seperation made the twins sad.
13 The lionness attacked the rhinoceros with incredible ferocity.
14 Political assasination is a heinous crime.

Score: /14

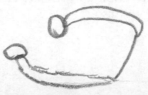

33

15   Some more troublesome nouns

A

Task 1

Complete each sentence by forming an appropriate noun from the adjective in brackets.

1 Her strange appearance aroused our .... (curious)
2 He has no sense of .... (responsible)
3 I like his sense of .... (humorous)
4 They have caused us a great deal of .... (anxious)
5 Does he have the .... and stamina to run a marathon? (strong)

Task 2

Complete each sentence by forming an appropriate noun (ending in *-sion* or *-ssion*) from the verb in brackets.

1 Do you have .... to be here? (permit)
2 There was a great deal of .... (confuse)
3 The vehicles were involved in a head-on .... (collide)
4 He was caught in .... of illegal drugs. (possess)
5 What was the cause of the .... ? (explode)
6 Are you going to do any .... for the exam? (revise)

Now check your answers and then consult the **Reference** section before going on to **B**.

Reference

a Note carefully the following spelling patterns (adjective - noun):
- gener*ous* - gener*os*ity; curi*ous* - curi*os*ity
- responsib*le* - responsib*il*ity; ab*le* - ab*il*ity
- hum*orous* - hum*our*; vig*orous* - vig*our*; glam*orous* - glam*our*
- an*xious* - an*xiety*; var*ious* - var*iety*
- lon*g* - len*gth*; stron*g* - stren*gth*

b Most nouns ending in *-ssion* are formed from verbs with the following endings:
- *-mit*: e.g. admit/admission; permit/permission; transmit/transmission
- *-cede* or *-ceed*: e.g. recede/recession; proceed/procession
- *-ss*: e.g. impress/impression; possess/possession

c Most nouns ending in *-sion* are formed from verbs with the following endings:

- *-de*: collide/collision; persuade/persuasion; provide/provision
- *-ere*: adhere/adhesion; cohere/cohesion
- *-nd*: expand/expansion; extend/extension; pretend/pretension
  (*Exceptions*: attend/attention; contend/contention;
  intend/intention)
- *-pel*: compel/compulsion; expel/expulsion; repel/repulsion
- *-use*: confuse/confusion; fuse/fusion
- *-vert*: convert/conversion; divert/diversion; pervert/perversion
- *-vise*: supervise/supervision; revise/revision

B

Task 1

Complete each sentence by forming an appropriate noun from the adjective in brackets.

1 We were impressed by his .... (generous)
2 He has the .... to do well in this subject. (able)
3 She expressed her opinions with great .... (vigorous)
4 It is said that .... is the spice of life. (various)
5 His problem is that he cannot concentrate for any .... of
   time. (long)   Score: /5

Task 2

Complete each sentence by forming an appropriate noun from the verb in brackets.

1   They are going to build an (extend) to the library.
2   In legal terms, a (confess) is an (admit) of guilt.
3   His (convert) to Buddhism surprised us.
4   Soil (erode) is a serious problem in many countries.
5   We were under the (impress) that you were not coming.
6   He has no (intend) of retiring.
7   I don't understand his (obsess) with golf.
8   Many companies go bankrupt during an economic (recede).
9   They lined the streets to watch the funeral (proceed).
10 They are building a (suspend) bridge.
11 He protested at his (exclude) from the team.
12 The teacher gave his students a (comprehend) test.
13 They tried to bomb the country into (submit).
14 She was threatened with (expel).
15 He had to do the work under close (supervise).
16 After a lot of (persuade), he agreed to come.
17 We apologise for the break in (transmit).
18 She created a (divert) while he stole the money.   Score: /19

16 Extending words of one syllable

A

Task

1 Add *-ed* to the words below and make any other necessary changes.
  spot - ban - tape - tap - row - cry - play - slap - pop - hum - peer - peep

2 Add *-ing* to the words below and make any other necessary changes.
  dig - slim - sweat - gaze - heat - hit - fly - shine - run - sew - stare - star

3 Add *-er* to the words below and make any other necessary changes.
  great - big - thin - fat - cool - mix - wet - wait - mug - rob - print

4 Add *-est* to the words below and make any other necessary changes.
  fast - sad - large - late - nice - dry - hot

5 Add *-en* to the words below and make any other necessary changes.
  deaf - rot - sad - wool - wood - mad - soft - glad

6 Add *-ish* to the words below and make any other necessary changes.
  red - snob - blue - fool - child

Now check your answers and then consult the **Reference** section before going on to **B**.

Reference

a We can extend a word by adding a suffix. Note what happens to words of one syllable when we add the following suffixes: *-ing*, *-ish*, *-ed*, *-er*, *-est*, *-en*.

- The final consonant is doubled if the base word has one vowel followed by one consonant.

e.g.   sit - sitting; fat - fatter; mad - madden; rub - rubbed; dim - dimmed
Exceptions: The letters *w*, *x* and *y* are never doubled.

e.g.   row - rowing; tax - taxed; play - played

- The final consonant is not doubled if the base word has two vowels followed by one consonant.

e.g.   steer - steering; hear - hearing; heat - heated; wood - wooden
Exception: wool - woollen

- If the base word ends in *-e*, the preceding consonant is not usually doubled.

e.g.   hope - hoped; phone - phoned; shine - shining; fine - finest
Don't forget *-e* disappears in front of a suffix beginning with *-i*.

e.g.   smile - smiling; take - taking; blue - bluish

36

- With words ending in a consonant + -y, the -y changes to -i when we add -er, -est or -ed.

e.g.   cry - cried; dry - drier

b Whenever you are in doubt as to whether to double a letter or to keep it single, apply the following pronunciation rule: one consonant follows a <u>long</u> vowel sound; two consonants follow a <u>short</u> vowel sound.

e.g.   later / the latter; writing / written; hoping (*hope*) / hopping (*hop*); biting / bitter / bitten; dinner-time / dining-room

B

Task 1   Add -*ing* to each word in brackets and make any other necessary changes.

1   He has to be on the (win) side. He hates being on the (lose) side.
2   Keep (stir) the soup for another minute.
3   Keep your hands on the (steer)-wheel!
4   I was (hope) that he would be in a better mood this afternoon, but he is still (hop) mad!
5   We are (write) to inform you that we are (plan) to take over your company.
6   We found him (sit) in the (dine)-room, (sob) his heart out.
7   Please stop (tap) your feet. And please stop (bite) your nails!
8   He spends Saturday afternoons (bet) on horses.
9   The sun was (shine), but it was (pour) with rain.   Score: /16

Task 2   Add -*ed* to the words in brackets and make any other necessary changes.

1   After the accident she was (scare) that she might be (scar) for life.
2   She (sneer) at him in a haughty manner, but he simply (grin) and (shrug) his shoulders.
3   He (fold) his arms and (nod) in agreement.
4   As he (step) forward, he (trip) over and fell flat on his face.
5   He (try) to hold it tight, but it (slip) out of his hands.
6   She (grab) the boy's hand and (drag) him up the stairs to the dentist's surgery.
7   We (wait) until he had (cool) down, and then we (beg) him not to leave.
8   The little child (yawn) and (rub) his sleepy eyes.
9   I (jot) down the information on a piece of scrap paper.   Score: /19

17 Extending words of more than one syllable

● ●

A

Task

1 Add *-ed* to the words below and make any other necessary changes.

commit - refer - offer - cancel - appeal - panic

2 Add *-ing* to the words below and make any other necessary changes.

prefer - quarrel - conceal - develop - benefit - begin

3 Add *-ence* to the words below and make any other necessary changes.

occur - refer - prefer - excel - differ

4 Add *-ation* to the words below and make any other necessary changes.

instal - cancel - imagine - limit - transport

Now check your answers and then consult the **Reference** section before going on to **B**.

Reference

a Many suffixes begin with a vowel: e.g. *-ed*, *-er*, *-ee*, *-ing*, *-ation*, *-able*, *-ence*. If we add any of these suffixes to a word of more than one syllable ending in one vowel + *-l*, the *-l* will double.

e.g.   quarrel - quarrelled - quarrelling; cancel - cancelled - cancellation

The letter *-l* does not double, however, if there are two vowels in front.

e.g.   conceal - concealed; reveal - revealing

b For all other words of more than one syllable ending in one vowel + consonant, we must apply the following rules:

● If the stress in pronunciation falls on the last syllable, then the final consonant is doubled if we add a suffix beginning with a vowel.

e.g.   regret - regretted - regrettable; begin - beginning

● If the stress does not fall on the last syllable, then the final consonant is not doubled.

e.g.   offer - offered; develop - developed; benefit - benefiting

● It is with words like *prefer* and *refer* that the stress rule is particularly important:

e.g.   prefer - preferred - preferring <u>but</u> preference - preferably; refer - referred <u>but</u> reference

Exceptions: handicap - handicapped; worship - worshipped - worshipping; kidnap - kidnapper - kidnapped - kidnapping (The *-p* is doubled in these three verbs even though the stress does not fall on the last syllable.)

c Note very carefully that the final consonant is not doubled if the suffix begins with a consonant.

e.g. fulfilment; commitment; quarrelsome

d Note that *-c* becomes *-ck* in such words as *panic* and *mimic*.

e.g. panicked, mimicking

e When a verb ends in *-qui* + consonant, we treat the *-ui* as a single vowel and apply the normal stress rules.

e.g. acquit - acquitted; equip - equipped

B

Task 1 Add *-ed* to each verb in brackets and make any other necessary changes.

1 I (order) a steak, not chicken!
2 It never (occur) to me that she might be lying.
3 She has (suffer) a great deal in her life.
4 He was (transfer) to another school.
5 He said that he (prefer) to be on his own.
6 They (enter) the room.
7 The horse (gallop) off into the distance.
8 His (handicap) daughter has been (kidnap).
9 She later (admit) that she (regret) her decision.
10 Nobody has (benefit) from the changes that have been made.
11 He has never (travel) abroad.
12 He then (reveal) who he really was.
13 I was (appal) by her behaviour.

Score: /15

Task 2 Extend each verb in brackets with the suffix at the end of the sentence.

1 What's (happen)? (*-ing*)
2 They are (question) him at this very moment. (*-ing*)
3 He left because he didn't find the job very (fulfil). (*-ing*)
4 The kitchen is (equip) with all the latest gadgets. (*-ed*)
5 We need to buy some more (equip). (*-ment*)
6 They are (instal) some new radiators. (*-ing*)
7 The first (instal) is due in February. (*-ment*)

Score: /7

18   Irregular verbs

A

Task 1

Supply the correct past form of each verb in brackets.

1 "I think I have (bring) the wrong tools with me," he (say).
2 The house was (build) over eighty years ago.
3 The doctors (fight) to save her life.
4 We (catch) the last bus home.
5 The ball (strike) him in the stomach.
6 If he had not (tread) on the scorpion, it would not have (bite) him.
7 It was the first time she had (ride) a horse and, fearing that she might be (throw) off, she (cling) to its neck as it (break) into a gallop.
8 Her faith in him had been (shake), and seeds of doubt had been (sow) in her mind.

Task 2

Correct the sentences below.

1 "I definitely seen her do it," he claimed.
2 "It's Mary's turn. I done the washing-up yesterday."
3 You should of seen his face!
4 She must of forgotten that we were having the meeting tonight.

Now check your answers and then consult the **Reference** section before going on to **B**.

Reference

a All regular verbs have just one past form (e.g. play - played). Many irregular verbs also have just one past form (e.g. hear - heard). In other words, with most verbs the simple past form and the past participle are one and the same.

Some irregular verbs, however, have two separate past forms: e.g. do - did (simple past) - done (past participle). In order to avoid confusing these two forms in your writing, it is important to understand what the past participle is used for.

b The past participle has four basic functions:

● It is used with the verb *to have* to form the 'perfect' tenses.

e.g.   I <u>have done</u> it. (= present perfect) / I <u>had seen</u> it before. (= past perfect)

- It is used with the verb *to have* to form a past infinitive.

e.g.   I should tell her. (*tell* = present infinitive) / I should <u>have told</u> her. (*have told* = past infinitive)

Note: In spoken English, the *have* of the past infinitive is often not fully pronounced and, therefore, sounds like *of*.

- It is used with the verb *to be* (and sometimes *to get*) when we wish to make a verb 'passive'.

e.g.   Ibrahim <u>was bitten</u> by the dog. = The dog bit Ibrahim.

- It can be used as an adjective.

e.g.   a <u>frozen</u> chicken, a <u>broken</u> toy

c   In standard English, it is wrong to use an irregular past participle as the main verb in a sentence. It is grammatically incorrect to write *he done it* or *she seen it*.

B

Task   Select the correct alternative in brackets.

1   The boat capsized and (sank / sunk) to the bottom of the lake.
2   We've (ran / run) out of sugar.
3   They (ran / run) out of the room and dashed up the stairs.
4   The choir (sang / sung) beautifully.
5   At the Olympic Games, the winner's national anthem is played but not (sang / sung).
6   We wanted to know where she had (hid / hidden) the money.
7   He has (forgot / forgotten) to order some spare parts.
8   I would (of / have) done it for you if you had asked me.
9   She wasn't there, so she couldn't (of / have) taken it.
10   Who's (took / taken) my book?
11   I think Rajendra (took / taken) it by mistake.
12   Our team's been (beat / beaten) again!
13   He's (fell / fallen) off his horse!
14   He was forty when he (came / come) out of the army.
15   I think he's (broke / broken) his leg.
16   She (broke / broken) the vase, so she will have to pay for it.
17   We couldn't read what he had (wrote / written).
18   The meeting (began / begun) at three and finished at five.
19   The meeting hasn't (began / begun) yet.
20   You (did / done) me a favour, so now I am going to help you.   Score: /20

Some tricky verbs

A

Select the correct alternative in brackets.

1 My mother told me to (lie / lay) down and get some sleep.
2 Our hens haven't (lain / laid) any eggs for days.
3 They have (raised / risen) his salary by 10 per cent.
4 His salary has (raised / risen) by 10 per cent.
5 My father is (teaching / learning) me to drive.
6 She (hung / hanged) the washing out on the line.
7 They (was / were) pleased to see us.
8 I wouldn't do that if I (was / were) you.
9 If she (doesn't / don't) behave, she will be punished.

Now check your answers and then consult the **Reference** section before going on to **B**.

Reference

a *lay* and *lie*

- *lay* is a transitive verb. This means it is always followed by an object noun or pronoun.

e.g.   A hen lays <u>eggs</u>.

- *lie* is an intransitive verb. This means it does not take an object. It is usually followed by a preposition.

e.g.   The village lies in a picturesque valley.

- The past form (and past participle) of *lay* is *laid*.

e.g.   They've just laid a new path in the garden.

- The past form of *lie* is *lay*.

e.g.   She lay down and tried to sleep.

- The past participle of *lie* is *lain*.

e.g.   His body had lain undiscovered in the forest for over a month.

- When *lie* means 'not to tell the truth', it has a different past form (= *lied*).

e.g.   I have never lied to you.

b *raise* and *rise*

- *raise* is a transitive verb. It requires an object.

e.g.   She raised <u>her voice</u>.

- *rise* is an intransitive verb. It does not take an object.

e.g. Her voice rose in anger.

c *teach* and *learn*

You <u>learn to do</u> something, but someone <u>teaches you to do</u> something.

d *hung* and *hanged*

We use *hanged* as the past form of *hang* when we are referring to someone being killed by means of hanging. In all other cases, we use *hung* as the past form of *hang*.

e *was* and *were*

- In written English we use *I*, *he*, *she*, *it* + <u>was</u>, and *we*, *you*, *they* + <u>were</u>.
- The only exception to the above is when we create <u>imaginary</u> situations with *if* and *wish*.

e.g. If only he were here. / I wish I were rich. / If I were you, I'd say nothing.

f *doesn't* and *don't*

Without exception, we use *he*, *she*, *it* + <u>doesn't</u>; and *I*, *we*, *you*, *they* + <u>don't</u>.

B

Task Select the correct alternative in brackets.

1 He said that he was just going to (lay / lie) down for a while.
2 Do you think you'll be able to (lay / lie) the carpet today?
3 He (lay / laid) a firm hand on my shoulder.
4 They found him (laying / lying) on the floor.
5 To cover their costs, they had to (raise / rise) their prices.
6 The price of popular toys always (raises / rises) just before Christmas.
7 My mum's been (learning / teaching) me to swim.
8 He was (hung / hanged) for murder.
9 I phoned to apologise but she just (hung / hanged) up on me.
10 We (was / were) pleased with the result.
11 They (was / were) surprised to find that I (was / were) from the same village.
12 "If I (was / were) you, I'd give up smoking," said the doctor.
13 "It (doesn't / don't) work," she complained.
14 "If she (doesn't / don't) turn up soon, we'll have to go without her," he said.

Score: /15

20   Some confusing words

A

Task 1

In each of the sentences below, there is one spelling mistake. Underline and correct each mistake.

1 The official gave us some very sensible advise.
2 She tries to practice the piano every day.
3 They were fined for not having a television license.
4 The police found an explosive devise in the bag.
5 It was humid and I found it difficult to breath.
6 I was advised to bath my eyes twice a day in warm water.

Task 2

Select the correct alternative in brackets.

1 There is no doubt that smoking (affects / effects) one's health.
2 The medicine had no (affect / effect) at all.
3 She didn't say anything because she didn't want to (lose / loose) her job.
4 Why did she (choose / chose) to wear that dress today?
5 He (assured / ensured) us that everything would be put right.
6 For how much have they (ensured / insured) the painting?
7 (Accept / Except) for John, the whole class went on the outing.

Now check your answers and then consult the **Reference** section before going on to **B**.

Reference

a To avoid confusion with certain words, you should remember that *s* means that the word is a <u>verb</u> (e.g. to advise, to practise, to license, to devise) and *c* means that the word is a <u>noun</u> (e.g. a piece of advice, hours of practice, a driving licence, a labour-saving device).

b *breath* is the noun form of the verb *to breathe*:

e.g.   She was out of breath.

c *bath* and *bathe* should be learnt in context:

- You take/have a bath; you bath a child.
- You bathe/go for a bathe in the sea; you bathe your eyes in water; you sunbathe.

d The verb *to affect* means 'to have an influence on', and *effect* is its noun form:

e.g.   It didn't affect me. / It had no effect on me.

e *to lose* is a verb:

e.g. Be careful not to lose it.

loose is an adjective, meaning 'not tight':

e.g. This screw is a bit loose.

f *chose* is the simple past form of the verb *to choose*

g Note how a different pattern follows the verbs *to ensure* and *to assure*:

You ensure <u>that</u> ... *but* You assure <u>someone</u> that ...

e.g. "Please ensure that this never happens again." (= Please make sure that ...) *but* "Let me assure you that this will never happen again." (= Let me tell you for certain that ...)

to insure = 'to take out insurance'

h *to accept* is a verb:

e.g. I accept what you say.

except (for) = 'apart from'

B

| Task |

Select the correct alternative in brackets.

1 I would strongly (advise / advice) you against doing that.
2 I found his (advise / advice) very useful.
3 You need more (practise / practice).
4 You need to (practise / practice) more.
5 It is a good theory, but will it work in (practise / practice)?
6 He was asked to produce his driving (license / licence).
7 This restaurant is fully (licensed / licenced).
8 We shall have to (devise / device) an alternative plan.
9 A computer is a (devise / device) for processing data.
10 When we (breath / breathe) in, we draw air into our lungs.
11 We went for a (bath / bathe) in the sea.
12 The changes did not (affect / effect) our department.
13 Her experiences abroad had a profound (affect / effect) on her.
14 This dress is too (lose / loose) around the waist.
15 He had to (chose / choose) between his family and his career.
16 It is his job to (assure / ensure) that everything is in place.
17 He (assured / ensured) her that he had tried his best.
18 I have (ensured / insured) the ring for £500.
19 They didn't (accept / except) our offer.

Score: /19

21 *-ible* and *-able*

A

| Task 1 | Choose the correct alternative in italics.

1 My uncle is a very *knowledgeable | knowledgable* person.
2 It did not have any *noticeable | noticable* effect.
3 She really is a most *disagreeable | disagreable* woman.
4 What he did was *unforgiveable | unforgivable*.
5 What an *adoreable | adorable* child!
6 What *unbelieveable | unbelievable* luck!
7 He gave the police some *valueable | valuable* information.
8 It was an *unforgetable | unforgettable* experience.

| Task 2 | Complete each word with either *-ible* or *-able*.

respons........... ; sens........... ; advis........... ; avail........... ; incred........... ;
irrit........... ; flex........... ; poss........... ; reli........... ; vis...........

Now check your answers and then consult the **Reference** section before going on to **B**.

Reference

a With or without *e*?

- You will never find *e* in front of *-ible*.
- We normally drop the *e* in front of *-able*.

e.g. adore - adorable; advise - advisable; forgive - forgivable

Exceptions (1): We usually keep the *e* with words that end in *-ce* or *-ge*.

e.g. notice - noticeable; knowledge - knowledgeable; change - changeable

(2): We keep the *e* if the word ends in *-ee*.

e.g. agree - agreeable; foresee - foreseeable

(3): In theory, we should drop the *e* when adding *-able* to the following words: *like, love, live, move, size*. In practice, it is entirely up to you whether to keep or drop the *e*. Thus: like - likable/likeable; love - lovable/loveable; live - livable/liveable; move - movable/moveable; size - sizable/sizeable.

b Single or double consonant?

Note carefully the spelling of the following words: forget + *-able* = *forgettable*; regret + *-able* = *regrettable*; prefer + *-able* = *preferable*; transfer + *-able* = *transferable*.

c *-ible* or *-able*?

There is no easy way of distinguishing between words ending in *-ible* and *-able*. You may, however, find the following guidelines useful:

- The vast majority of words will end in *-able*. Treat those that end in *-ible* as exceptions.

- Base words that are complete (or almost complete) in themselves tend to take *-able*.

e.g.   accept - acceptable; avoid - avoidable

- Words that can take the suffix *-ion* will very often take *-ible*.

e.g.   divide - division - divisible; vision - visible;
comprehension - comprehensible

- Very often *-ible* follows *-s*.

e.g.   sensible; possible; responsible

- Never place *-ible* after a vowel.

e.g.   reliable; viable; sociable

B

Task 1 | Choose the correct alternative in italics.

1   The weather in Britain is notoriously *changeable | changable*.
2   He is suffering from an *incureable | incurable* disease.
3   Such behaviour is *inexcuseable | inexcusable*.
4   What he did was most *regretable | regrettable*.
5   This ticket is not *transferable | transferrable*.
6   Be careful with this Ming vase. It's *irreplaceable | irreplacable*.
7   I knew it was him. His voice is *unmistakeable | unmistakable*.

Score: /7

Task 2 | Where a word is incomplete, complete it with either *-ible* or *-able*.

1   The heat was unbear.................. .
2   He is very soci.................. .
3   No army is invinc.................. .
4   The word *dinosaur* actually means 'terr.................. lizard'.
5   They said it was imposs.................. to do that.
6   The delay was unavoid.................. .
7   The food was horr.................. . In fact, it was ined.................. .
8   Be careful. That material is inflamm.................. .
9   His writing is illeg.................. .

Score: /10

22 -*ent* and -*ant*

A

Task

Where a word is incomplete, complete it with either -*ent* or -*ant*.

1   I hate feeling depend.................. on others.
2   He said that his elderly mother was his only depend.................. .
3   Australia is an independ.................. nation.
4   She claims to be a direct descend.................. of Queen Victoria.
5   He said he was not interested in curr.................. affairs.
6   A cloakroom attend.................. took my coat.
7   That's not relev.................. to our discussion!
8   She was most insist.................. on that point.
9   How did the accid.................. happen?
10 He doesn't sound very confid.................. .
11 He is extremely arrog.................. .
12 This material is fire-resist.................. .
13 There has been a signific.................. increase in burglaries.
14 She is flu.................. in five languages.

Now check your answers and then consult the **Reference** section before going on to **B**.

Reference

a   Certain words may end in either -*ent* or -*ant*.

- (in)dependent (an adjective); a dependant (a noun)
- a currant (a fruit); a current (a flow of air, water, electricity); the current climate (*current* = 'of the present time')

b   Apart from the examples given above and a few other words, it is not easy to distinguish between -*ent* and -*ant* because they invariably sound the same, and either ending can denote a noun or an adjective.

c   It is best to learn the most common words by heart as you come across them. It is, however, well worth knowing a few rules of thumb concerning the use of -*ent* and -*ant*.

- A noun that describes what somebody does in terms of a job or a trade will usually end in -*ant*.

e.g.   assistant, attendant, accountant, servant

On the other hand, if the noun has a soft *g* it will end in -*ent*.

e.g.   agent, regent

- The last point mentioned above also applies to adjectives. A soft *g* tells us the ending will be *-ent*, and a hard *g* tells us that the ending will be *-ant*.

e.g.   diligent, intelligent *but* elegant, arrogant, extravagant

- Likewise, *-ent* will follow a soft *c*, and *-ant* will follow a hard *c*.

e.g.   decent, recent *but* significant, vacant

- *-ent* usually follows certain letter combinations:

(i) *-cid-, -fid-, -sid-, -vid-*

e.g.   incident, confident, resident, president, evident

(ii) *-flu-, -qu-*

e.g.   fluent, frequent

(iii) *-sist-*

e.g.   consistent, insistent

Exceptions: assistant, resistant

B

| Task | Where a word is incomplete, complete it with either *-ent* or *-ant*. |

1   He made himself a cup of inst.............. coffee.
2   He looks really eleg.............. in his new suit.
3   The strong curr.............. carried the boat downstream.
4   She is a persist.............. tru.............. .
5   We spent a pleas.............. day in the countryside.
6   She was reluct.............. to admit that she was wrong.
7   The police are investigating the incid.............. .
8   The view from the top was magnific.............. .
9   I am looking for a perman.............. job.
10   The matter is extremely urg.............. .
11   Your work is excell.............. .
12   You think he's brilli..............; I think he's ignor..............!
13   Is this a conveni.............. moment?
14   The hospital holds special classes for expect.............. mothers.
15   He knows some of the most emin.............. scientists in Europe.
16   He thanked her for the pres.............. .
17   That was very observ.............. of you.
18   There was one applic.............. for the vac.............. post.
19   He was told not to be so insol.............. .
20   The judge decided to be leni.............. .
21   She asked if they had any blackcurr.............. jam.
22   We are almost totally reli.............. on imported oil.   Score: /25

23 Negative prefixes

A

Task 1

Choose the correct alternative in italics.

1 He is sometimes *inattentive | innattentive* in class.
2 That was *irresponsible | iresponsible* of her.
3 She found him totally *irresistible | iresistible*.
4 He was *disappointed | dissappointed* with his exam results.
5 These spaces are reserved for *dissabled | disabled* drivers.
6 She said that she was *dissatisfied | disatisfied* with his work.
7 I hope you will not *mispell | misspell* this word!
8 That is not true. You have been *missinformed | misinformed*.
9 It was *unecessary | unnecessary* to do that.
10 He is very *imature | immature* for his age.
11 Her handwriting is *ilegible | illegible*.
12 What he did was *illegal | ilegal*.

Task 2

Complete the sentences below by using the words given in italics.

misused | disused | unused

1 The old, ... church was converted into a family home.
2 Here's a(n) .... envelope. Will it do?
3 They claimed that he had .... his authority.

uninterested | disinterested

4 During the dispute he claimed to be a(n) .... observer, but we soon found out where his true interests lay.
5 I thought he might like to play some games on the computer, but he looked totally .... when I suggested the idea.

Now check your answers and then consult the **Reference** section before going on to **B**.

Reference

a Some words seem very difficult to spell at first sight, but are actually fairly straightforward once you realise that they consist of a negative prefix and a whole word.

 dis- + satisfied = dissatisfied; *dis-* + appointed = disappointed

b Look carefully at the list of negative prefixes below and the examples alongside.

im-:   *im-* + moral = immoral; *im-* + possible = impossible; *im-* + polite = impolite

in-:   *in-* + numerable = innumerable; *in-* + accurate = inaccurate

ir-:   *ir-* + resistible = irresistible; *ir-* + rational = irrational

il-:   *il-* + literate = illiterate; *il-* + logical = illogical

un-:   *un-* + natural = unnatural; *un-* + occupied = unoccupied

dis-:   *dis-* + appear = disappear; *dis-* + organised = disorganised

mis-:   *mis-* + spell = misspell; *mis-* + place = misplace

c The general meaning of a negative prefix is 'not' or 'opposite of'. Be careful, however, with certain words that can take different negative prefixes with different shades of meaning.

e.g.   (1) misused = 'used wrongly, badly' (e.g. the misuse of power); disused = 'no longer being used' (e.g. a disused mine); unused = 'not having been used' (e.g. an unused stamp); unused to = 'unaccustomed to'

(2) disinterested = 'neutral, impartial'; uninterested = 'not interested'

B

Task 1   Add a suitable negative prefix to each word.

1	.............patient	8	.............polite
2	.............considerate	9	.............mortal
3	.............appear	10	.............replaceable
4	.............lead	11	.............efficient
5	.............respectful	12	.............approve
6	.............relevant	13	.............behave
7	.............grateful	14	.............honest

Score: /14

Task 2   Select the correct alternative in italics.

1 She did not want to *dissapoint | disappoint* her parents.
2 This report is *unnofficial | unofficial*.
3 He slipped into the house *unnoticed | unoticed*.
4 She *dissagreed | disagreed* with what he said.
5 Why did the soldiers *dissobey | disobey* the order?
6 *Iregular | Irregular* verbs should be learnt by heart.
7 They discovered that he was *iliterate | illiterate*.
8 It is *inadvisable | innadvisable* to take a bath straight after a meal.
9 He said the charity's funds were being *missused | misused*.
10 He was accused of being *dissloyal | disloyal*.

Score: /10

24 Adverbs

● ●

A

Task 1

Read the following letter from a teacher to one of her pupils. As you read the letter, select the correct alternative in brackets.

Dear June,

I am just writing to say how (terribley / terribly) sorry I was to hear about your pet dog, Fruno.

You must be (dreadfuly / dreadfully) upset, (especialy / especially) since it was your own father who (accidently / accidentally) drove over the dog while backing his car out of the garage.

(Unfortunately / Unfortunatley), the school does not offer counselling sessions for the type of tragedy that you have suffered.

I shall (fuly / fully) understand if you decide to take a few weeks off school to recover from your shock.

With my very best wishes,

Yours (sincerely / sincerelly),

Janet Barker

PS It (usualy / usually) takes between one and three months for a broken leg to heal (properley / properly). So, quite (possibley / possibly), Fruno will be walking again within a short time. Fingers crossed!

Task 2

Look at the words that have been underlined in the sentences below. If the word is written correctly, tick it. If the word is grammatically wrong, correct it.

1 Try to work as <u>fast</u> as you can. 2 Try to work as <u>quick</u> as you can.
3 As the road was slippery, he drove <u>careful</u> and <u>slow</u>. 4 He asked her to keep <u>quiet</u>. 5 He shut the door <u>quiet</u>. 6 She plays football as <u>good</u> as any of the boys in the class. 7 They were supposed to be a <u>strong</u> team, but we beat them <u>easy</u>. 8 She looked rather <u>anxious</u>. 9 She looked <u>anxious</u> at her brother. 10 She finds it very difficult to write <u>neat</u>.

Now check your answers and then consult the **Reference** section before going on to **B**.

Reference

Many adverbs end in *-ly* (e.g. greatly, really), but some do not (e.g. so, too, quite).

a Using adverbs:

- We use adverbs with 'active' verbs (= 'doing' words) to show, for example, how something is being done.

e.g. He drove slowly. / She sings beautifully.

- An adverb is also used to give extra information about an adjective or another adverb. An adverb can also be an independent phrase commenting on a whole sentence.

e.g. She is really nice. / She spoke <u>too</u> quickly. / <u>Luckily</u>, nobody was injured.

- We use an <u>adjective</u> – not an adverb – with 'non-active' verbs that describe appearance, a state or condition (= what someone/something is like).

e.g. That looks interesting. / That smells delicious. / He seems nice.

- We use adjectives instead of adverbs in certain fixed phrases.

e.g. keep quiet / open wide / hold tight

- The adverbial form of *good* is *well*. Some words (e.g. fast, late, hard) function as adjectives and adverbs.

e.g. He did well. / He arrived late. / She worked hard.

b Forming adverbs ending in *-ly*:

An adverb is formed from an adjective. Take the full form of the adjective and apply the following rules:

- For most words, add *-ly* (even when the word already ends in an *-l*).

e.g. real - really; accidental - accidentally; normal - normally

Note: If the word ends in *-ll*, just add *-y*: e.g. full - fully

- The final *-e* of an adjective is not usually dropped.

e.g. rare - rarely

Exceptions (1): true - truly; due - duly; whole - wholly
　　　　　　(2): If a word ends in a consonant + *-le* (e.g. *-ble*, *-dle*), drop the *-e* and add only *-y*.

e.g. terrible - terribly; idle - idly

- If a word ends in a consonant + *-y*, drop the *-y* and add *-ily*.

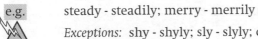

e.g. steady - steadily; merry - merrily

Exceptions: shy - shyly; sly - slyly; dry - dryly (*or* drily)

- After *-ic*, the ending is *-ally*.

e.g. basic - basically

Exception: publicly

Read the letter below. Turn each adjective in brackets into an adverb.

Dear Mr Smithson,

Please accept my apologies for the unpardonable delay in answering your letter of 16 May. (Unfortunate), my secretary was off sick for nearly two months and, most (regrettable), her temporary replacement proved to be (extreme) unreliable. In fact, she was (utter) incompetent.

It was not until my regular secretary returned that your letter was discovered — together with thirty others — locked away in a drawer. Such things do (occasional) occur even in the most efficient of companies, and once again I wish to say how (true) sorry I am.

In your letter you ask for details of our course on 'How to become a millionaire'. Please send me £50 (immediate) and I shall (glad) provide you with your first lesson.

In the meantime, I (humble) beg you to reflect on the following testimonial from a client who has (happy) parted with £50 in order to enrol on our (incredible) successful course for potential millionaires:

'This is (simple) the best get-rich-quick scheme on the market. I know that I will (easy) get my money back — and more. For example, I was paid £15 to give this testimonial. That shows that this scheme (real) does work.' — Sidney, Sussex.

I look forward to receiving your cheque or postal order.

Yours (sincere),

Max Smart

Max Smart

Score: /15

Making comparisons

. . . .

A

Task 1 Look at the pairs of sentences below. In each case, one of the sentences has a grammatical error. The other sentence is grammatically correct. Find the error and correct it.

1 a He is the most cleverest person I have ever met.
   b She is cleverer than you think.
2 a My cold is getting worse.
   b Honestly, it was the worse day of my life.
3 a Ivan is undoubtedly the best player in the team.
   b If I have to choose between Ahmed and Tariq, I think Ahmed is the best player.
4 a The patient recovered quicker than expected.
   b The patient's recovery was quicker than expected.
5 a You should eat less chocolate and fewer biscuits.
   b There have been far less burglaries in this area this year than there were last year.
6 a They are as different as chalk from cheese.
   b The film is completely different than the book.

Task 2 Correct any spelling mistakes in the sentences below.

1 It was the funneyest thing I had ever seen. 2 Better late then never! 3 He said it would be much cooller in here, but actually it's much hotter here than where we were before. 4 The riper the fruit, the tastyer it usually is. 5 The earlyer we begin, the sooner we will be able to finish.

Now check your answers and then consult the **Reference** section before going on to **B**.

Reference

a Comparatives and superlatives

- When we say *smaller*, we are using the <u>comparative</u> form of *small*. When we say *smallest* we are using the <u>superlative</u> form of *small*.
- We use the comparative form of a word to make a comparison <u>between one</u> person/group/item/situation <u>and another</u> person/group/item/situation.

e.g. She is taller than her brother. / He took the bigger piece. / It will be quicker by train than by bus.

- We normally use *than* to join the two halves of a comparison. Note, however, that we say that one person/item is *different from* another person/item.

- We use *fewer* – not *less* – with plural nouns.

e.g. There are fewer people here today than there were yesterday.

We use *less* with singular nouns.

e.g. A shower uses less water than a bath.

- We use the superlative form of a word when we wish to select <u>one</u> person/item <u>from</u> a group.

e.g. She is the tallest in the class. / He is the eldest of the three.

b Forming comparatives and superlatives

It is important not to confuse adjectives and adverbs when making comparisons.

- For most adverbs (ending in *-ly*), we use *more* (= comparative) and *most* (= superlative).

e.g. He asked her to drive more carefully. / Please speak more slowly.

- For one-syllable adjectives, add *-er* or *-est*. (See also Unit 16.)

e.g. big - bigger - biggest; clean - cleaner - cleanest

- For adjectives of two syllables ending in consonant + *-y*, drop the *-y* and add *-ier* or *-iest*.

e.g. pretty - prettier - prettiest; easy - easier - easiest

- For certain two-syllable adjectives (e.g. narrow, simple, common, clever), we can use *-er* and *-est*.

e.g. simple - simpler - simplest

- For all other long-sounding adjectives of two syllables or more, we use *more* and *most*.

e.g. intelligent - more intelligent - most intelligent

- Certain adverbs and adjectives share the same comparative and superlative form.

e.g. good/well - better - best; bad/badly - worse - worst; fast - faster - fastest; early - earlier - earliest; soon - sooner - soonest; late - later - latest; hard - harder - hardest

B

Complete the sentences below with the correct alternative given in italics.

neater | more neatly
1   The teacher asked her to write ....
2   Her handwriting is .... than mine.

less | fewer
3   His dentist told him to eat .... sweets in future.
4   In the examination, he should have spent .... time on Section A.
5   There are .... candidates for the exam this year.

better | best
6   Of the two, Elena is the .... linguist.
7   Elena is the .... linguist this school has ever produced.
8   It was a close match, but there is no doubt that the .... team won.

worse | worst
9   His bark is .... than his bite.
10 I reckon I am .... off than before.
11 Marrying him was the .... thing she could possibly have done.   Score: /11

Task 2 Write out the correct comparative/superlative form of each word in brackets.

1   Derek is definitely the (lazy) boy in the class!
2   I do a lot of exercise. That's why I am (healthy) and (fit) than you are.
3   She asked the children to play (quiet) as they were making too much noise.
4   Of the four brothers, Naseer is certainly the (good)-looking but by no means is he the (clever).
5   This new machine works (efficient) than the old one.
6   You are too slow. You are the (slow) in the class. You need to learn to work (quick).
7   He arrived (early) than the others.   Score: /10

26 'as' and 'like'

A

In spoken English we tend to use *as* and *like* rather loosely. In informal speech we often use *like* in preference to *as*. In written English, however, we should show that we are aware of the rules that govern the standard use of these two words.

| Task 1 | Fill in each gap below with *as* or *like*. |

1 Do .... you are told!
2 He is .... his father in many ways.
3 She ran .... the wind.
4 She was dressed exactly .... I was.
5 When in Rome, do .... the Romans do.
6 She is acting .... my guardian until my parents return.
7 .... you know, Mr Brown is retiring soon.
8 He used the bad weather .... an excuse not to come.
9 We're going to Spain, ... we do every summer.
10 .... I said in my letter, I can't help you.

| Task 2 | Fill in each gap below with *like* or *as if*. |

1 It looks .... rain.
2 It looks .... it is going to rain.
3 Please stop treating me .... I were a five-year-old!
4 Would you stop treating me .... a five-year-old!
5 You look .... you have been crying.

Now check your answers and then consult the **Reference** section before going on to **B**.

Reference

a When choosing between *as* and *like*, it is important to remember that we do not use *like* before a clause (= subject + verb) in standard written English.

☒ Like I said last week, I won't be able to attend the next meeting.
☑ As I said last week, I won't be able to attend the next meeting.

b When talking about the similarity between people, things and actions, we use either *as* or *like*.

- *like* is used before a noun or pronoun.

e.g.   He works too hard, (just) like his father. / She swims like a fish.

- *as* is used before a clause or a preposition.

e.g.   He works too hard, (just) as his father did. / In Central America, as in most parts of South America, Spanish is the official language.

c   When defining the function, purpose, occupation or role of a person or thing, we use *as* + noun.

e.g.   She managed to get a job as a teacher.

d   In situations where we want to say what something <u>seems</u> like, we use *like* + noun and *as if* (or *as though*) + clause.

e.g.   Stop acting like a fool! / She looked as if she had been crying.

e   Certain verbs (e.g. describe, regard) automatically take *as*.

e.g.   I regard her as my best friend.

With other verbs, the use of *as* or *like* will depend on exactly what you want to say.

e.g.   He uses the family home like a hotel. (= He treats the family home as if it were a hotel.) / He wants to use the family home as a hotel. (= He wants to turn the family home into a hotel.)

f   We also use *as* with expressions of certainty and agreement.

e.g.   As you know, we ... / As we agreed last week, we ...

B

Task

Fill in each gap with *as*, *as if* or *like*.

1   He treats me .... an idiot.
2   It looks .... we are going to be late again!
3   Nobody understands me .... my mother does.
4   His career .... a professional footballer is over.
5   He works .... a dog.
6   He works .... a waiter.
7   A frog starts life .... a tadpole.
8   They say she drinks .... a fish.
9   She got the job, ... I thought she would.
10   He looked at me .... I were mad.
11   She behaved .... nothing had happened.
12   .... you can see, my hands are empty.
13   She looked .... she had just seen a ghost.
14   He was treated .... a king when he won the lottery.   Score: /14

27 Words that sound alike

A

Task

Choose the correct alternative in brackets.

1 She is (to / two / too) clever by half!
2 I can't bake a cake because I have run out of (flour / flower).
3 He is the (principle / principal) of a language school.
4 Oysters are more expensive than (mussels / muscles).
5 You will find the gas (metre / meter) in the basement.
6 She walked (passed / past) me without saying a word.
7 Could you close the door? (There's / Theirs) a (draft / draught) in (here / hear).
8 He asked me (which / witch) one I preferred.
9 She had a (horse / hoarse) voice after speaking (for / four) so long.
10 She has forgotten to sign the (check / cheque).
11 Why do you want to (dye / die) your (hair / hare) (blue / blew)?
12 You reap what you (sew / so / sow).
13 I think you should dress more (formerly / formally).
14 I don't mean to be rude, but I think (you're / your) putting on (weight / wait).
15 My (father / farther) keeps his (whine / wine) down in the (seller / cellar).
16 Spiders (pray / prey) on small flies.
17 Would you like some breakfast (serial / cereal)?
18 How much is the bus (fare / fair)?
19 On the (hole / whole), I am very pleased with your work.
20 The soldiers were ordered to shoot on (site / sight).

Now check your answers and then consult the **Reference** section before going on to **B**.

Reference

a Words that sound the same are known as *homophones* (from the Greek for 'same sound'). The spelling of these words depends on the context in which they are found. In other words, never rely just on the sound of a word when checking your spelling. For example, *great* and *grate* are pronounced the same, and this causes problems with the word *grateful* (which students often misspell as *greatful*). When in doubt, consult a dictionary.

b The existence of homophones in the English language has given rise to a type of humour that is peculiarly British: the pun, or play on words. Here are some examples:

- A teacher saw two boys fighting in the playground.
  "Stop!" he shouted. "You know the rules: no fighting *allowed*!"
  "But, sir, we weren't fighting *aloud*. We were fighting quietly."

- "Waiter, what do you call this?"
  "It's *bean* soup, sir."
  "I don't care what it's *been*. What is it now?"

B

| Task |

Select the correct alternative in brackets.

1   I am tired. Let's have a (break / brake).
2   I'll (wring / ring) his neck when I see him!
3   The (reign / rein / rain) in Spain falls mainly on the (plane / plain).
4   You can buy (stationery / stationary) at that shop.
5   (Who's / Whose) book is this?
6   I'm afraid (their / there / they're) not ready yet. Can you wait?
7   Would you like a (piece / peace) of cake?
8   She was forced to (flee / flea) the country.
9   I didn't know (whether / weather) to tell her or not.
10 Thank you for the (complement / compliment).
11 It is a five-(story / storey) building.
12 There is a limit to my (patience / patients)!
13 The dog wagged (it's / its) (tail / tale) and held out a (poor / pore / pour / paw).
14 That particular pop-star is her (idle / idol).
15 He has a (soar / sore / saw) throat.
16 They crossed the (boarder / border) late at (night / knight).
17 He was the (soul / sole) survivor.
18 (Heroin / Heroine) is a highly addictive and dangerous drug.
19 The author asked the distinguished professor to (right / write / rite) a (foreword / forward) to his new book.
20 They walked (threw / through) the forest.
21 We need to (altar / alter) the schedule.
22 Aeroplanes are kept in (hangers / hangars).
23 At the end of the service, they sang a well-known (him / hymn).
24 He was admitted to hospital for some (minor / miner) surgery.
25 He tried to (prise / prize) open the box with a knife.

Score: /30

28   Silent letters

A

Task 1

Each of the words below contains a silent letter (= a letter that is not pronounced). Pronounce each word and, in each case, underline the silent letter.

write - watch - scientist - numb - character - guard - knot - salmon - campaign - autumn - listen - island - honest - biscuit - adjacent

Task 2

Carefully read the sentences below. How many spelling mistakes can you find in each sentence?

1   He took out his hankerchief and rapped it around his injured rist.
2   She said she woud never forget the day she became officially engaged: Wensday 22 Febuary.
3   On the day of her marrige, she was driven to church in a horse-drawn carrige.
4   The nauty boy stuk his thum in a plum.
5   They thout it would be a good idea if the goverment created an agency with overall responsibility for the enviroment.
6   She asked him if he wanted a cheese omlette, but he said he'd rather have a ham sanwich.
7   Anybody who wants to see a sychiatrist should have his head examined!
8   They feched some rope and then climed to the top of the tower.
9   The chairperson decided to ajourn the meeting before it ended in caos.
10   My father is a bucher and my uncle is a plumer.

Now check your answers and then consult the **Reference** section before going on to **B**.

Reference

As we saw in the previous unit, the sound of a word in English does not necessarily indicate how that word will be spelt. This is particularly true of words with silent letters.

Note carefully the following examples of words with silent letters:

carriage, marriage (= *a*); climber, plumber, doubt, debt (= *b*); scientist, conscious, acquire, acquaint (= *c*); judge, hedge, adjust, adjourn (= *d*);

shone, axe, engine (= *e*); gnaw, campaign (= *g*); weight, height, taught (= *gh*); character, ache, honour, rhyme (= *h*); knot, knuckle (= *k*); could, would, salmon, calm, half, calf (= *l*); autumn, solemn, government, environment (= *n*); pneumonia, psychology, receipt (= *p*); island, isle (= *s*); castle, listen, fetch, catch (= *t*); guard, guarantee (= *u*); write, wrong, sword, answer (= *w*)

B

Task

Read the joke below. How many spelling mistakes (involving silent letters) can you find?

"Has Simon got long to live?" Robert asked the nurse.

"I don't no," she replied. "Shall I fech the doctor?"

"Please," insisted Robert in a solem voice.

The doctor arrived some minutes later.

"Sorry to have kept you waiting, but I was stiching up one of my patients," he explained.

Robert came strait to the point: "How bad is it? How long has Simon got to live?"

"Not long, I'm afraid. He coud die at any moment," the doctor ansered. "He's barely consious."

On hearing the bad news, Robert went immediately to see Simon, his frend and busness partner.

Simon was lying in bed, and he was so weak that he coud hardly speak. When he saw Robert sitting beside him, he raised his head from the pillow and began to wisper: "Robert... Robert..."

"Rest, Simon, rest," Robert advised, noting how gastly white Simon's skin had turned. "Save your strenth."

"No," insisted the dying man. "I can't. I must clear my consience before I die."

"What's troubling you, Simon?" asked Robert, scraching his head.

"I have been a very bad partner, Robert. I have been disloyal to you. Do you know how I aquired my Mercedes? Well, I stole £50,000 from the office safe. And do you remember when you were taken to court for not having paid any tax for ten years? You were aquitted on a technicality, if you remember. Well, I was the one who reported you to the tax inspector. I was the one who told your wife about you and the blonde secretry. I was the one who..."

"Don't worry, Simon," replied Robert, neeling down beside him. "Please, don't worry. I was the one who put poison in your cup of tea."

Score: /20

Some problems of usage

A

Task 1

Select the correct alternative in brackets.

1 I was surprised at the (amount / number) of mistakes he made.
2 She does not have the right qualifications for the job, (beside / besides) which she is far too young.
3 Both John and Peter are suitable for the job, but the (later / latter) has slightly better qualifications.
4 I was interviewed by the (personal / personnel) manager.
5 He is a very (imaginary / imaginative) writer.

Task 2

Look at the words that have been underlined. Have they been used correctly? Make any necessary corrections.

1 He said that there was no <u>historic</u> evidence for her theory.
2 This particular car is fairly <u>economic</u> on fuel.
3 The fire was caused by an <u>electric</u> fault.
4 'High Noon' is a <u>classical</u> western. It is a brilliant cowboy film.
5 I can't work with these <u>continuous</u> interruptions!
6 I loved the film, <u>specially</u> the last part.

Now check your answers and then consult the **Reference** section before going on to **B**.

Reference

There are many pairs or groups of words in the English language which closely resemble one another in appearance or meaning, and consequently are easily confused. You will already have come across many examples of confusing pairs in various parts of this book. Now carefully study the following list:

a The word *number* implies a group of separate items: e.g. a number of students/chairs/pens. The word *amount* implies a mass, and is used with 'uncountable' nouns: e.g. a particular amount of time/work/sugar/flour.

b *beside* = 'next to'; *besides* = 'in addition to', 'apart from'

c *later*: the comparative of *late*; *the latter* = 'the second of two persons or items that have just been mentioned'

d *personal* = 'private'; *personnel* = 'staff in a company or business'

e *imaginary* = 'not real'; *imaginative* = 'showing great imagination'

f *historic* = 'important', 'significant in history' (e.g. a historic moment/building); *historical* = 'concerning past events' (e.g. historical research/facts)

g *economical* = 'not expensive', 'not wasteful'; *economic* = 'to do with the economy' (e.g. the government's economic policies)

h *electric* = 'powered by electricity' (e.g. an electric fire/cooker/heater); *electrical*: a more general adjective (e.g. an electrical engineer/appliance/fault)

i *classic* = 'of particularly high quality, a good example of its kind' (e.g. This record is a classic.), 'very typical' (e.g. a classic example/mistake); *classical* = 'serious and traditional in style' (e.g. classical music)

j *continual* describes something that happens repeatedly; *continuous* = 'unbroken', 'without interruption'

k *especially* = 'in particular', 'above all'; *specially* indicates a specific purpose (e.g. I came here specially to see you.)

B

Task 1 Select the correct alternative in brackets.

1 This cake was (specially / especially) made for you.
2 You will find the case (beside / besides) the wardrobe.
3 "Your fears are (imaginary / imaginative)," he said.
4 "I'll see you (later / latter)," he said.
5 Education is a (continual / continuous) process.
6 She is studying (classical / classic) and modern ballet.
7 We need to find a more (economic / economical) way of heating this building.
8 All the newspapers described the meeting of the two presidents as a (historic / historical) occasion.
9 Those letters are (personal / personnel).   Score: /9

Task 2 Choose the correct alternative.

1 Are you (quite / quiet) sure you know what you are doing?
2 Could you show me (where / were) you found the object?
3 What shall we have for (desert / dessert)?
4 Do you have a spare (envelop / envelope)?
5 The team will (consist / comprise) of the following: Mark, John, ...
6 The house was struck by (lightening / lightning).
7 You should learn to be more (tolerable / tolerant) of others.
8 You are too (trusting / trustworthy). That's why people take advantage of you.
9 I am feeling rather (alone / lonely).   Score: /9

30   Common spelling errors

A

Task 1

How many spelling mistakes are there in the jokes below?

a   Ron: What's your New Year's resolution?
     Bert: To be much less concieted.
     Ron: Won't that be dificult to maintain for a year?
     Bert: Not for someone as clever and inteligent as me.

b   "I don't like cabbige, and I'm glad I don't like it. If I did like it,
     I'd eat it – and I hate the stuff!"

Task 2

The words in italics have been misspelt. Correct them.

1   What is your *adress*?
2   It was an *exiting* game of football.
3   He said he would *deffinately* be coming to the party.
4   She asked the receptionist for an *emergancy apointment*.
5   The *parrott* nibbled on a *carott*.
6   He was too *embarassed* to say anything.
7   He was asked if he could *reccommend* a good school.
8   When she heard the news, she *imedietley* phoned her mother.
9   Did she get the *messige*?
10   The whole class was *punnished*.

Now check your answers and then consult the **Reference** section before going on to **B**.

Reference

Certain words cause more spelling problems than others. You should
get into the habit of grouping the most troublesome ones together –
and then learn them by heart. Note carefully the word groups below.

a   *ie/ei*: The basic rule is '*i* before *e* except after *c* when the sound is *ee*'.

e.g.   <u>Group 1</u>: conceited, receive, receipt, deceive
       <u>Group 2</u>: believe, relief, chief

     ●   There are, however, exceptions to the rule:

e.g.   seize, Neil, Sheila, Keith

     ●   There are also other words that should be learnt separately:

e.g.   foreign, friend, leisure, neither